Our Father
Whom Is in
HEAVEN

J.L Mclaurin

ISBN 978-1-64258-243-7 (paperback)
ISBN 978-1-64258-245-1 (hardback)
ISBN 978-1-64258-244-4 (digital)

Christian Faith Publishing, Inc.
832 Park Avenue
Meadville, PA 16335
www.christianfaithpublishing.com

Printed in the United States of America

Dedicated to our Father who is truly in heaven.

J.L. McLaurin

Thank you
for your
kindness

Introduction

I want to give you the highest praise for a legacy of family in your Holy Bible and life, health, and strength. I can never repay you for all your mighty deeds done in my life, so I write in your honor until the day I die. Thank you, precious Father. And thanking you for my mother, Mary Louise Hinton-McLaurin, a true treasure that you loaned to me for a little while. She was the one who introduced me to you. Thanks, Mom, for your dedication to our God, family, and friends. I thank our Father after thinking about this for decades. I've decided to show honor to our only Father in heaven. I believe that God is our only Father. And man the human being is not made by man's hands, but every human being on earth is made by God. And every human being comes from above. Born to man and woman. But approved with the stamp of love before entering the realm of earth. I believe we are not from earth originally, but from above from the start—a spirit. We were made human to fulfill our goals and tasks on this earthly test. It is a test. And in the end, we, as human beings, either pass or fail. And we go to hell or heaven. It's a hearing, learning, and seeing experience.

We must study and seek our Father with all our might. We must study his Holy Word. We are ordered to do so in his Holy Word, the book of Acts 10 and 42, men on earth are not fathers, they are guardians. And dads—they are protector and men that feed and clothe children, but we, as human beings, have only one Father. And he is in heaven. We, as people, got it all wrong. Our Father in heaven has no stepchildren. If a man or woman does the best that they can every day of their life if a man works hard for his family. If a man loves God first and lives an empowered life and starves to death. And begs for food every day like millions of people around the world every day. And feeds his hungry children who are hungry as well, and that man or woman starves to death doing the best that they can day in and day out obeying God's Word. I believe they will make heaven their eternal home. And if a man or woman becomes billionaires doing their own will and ignores our Father's will, I believe they will spend eternity in hell.

The people have choices in this lifetime, very hard choices, during very difficult times. The time is now to do what is right. It truly is a hard every-day fight from the time you hit the floor all through the place you live to the exit door. To the porch to the streets to the people you meet. Every one you meet has a problem from money to drugs to gang wars to fights to spite to jails and to each one's wife. To running and crying to people dying. There are many ways to getting in trouble. The two that I know for sure is starting and stopping. I would like to explore life with you from many points of view.

Starting with Adam and Eve. Neither of these people were born. Adam was created from the dust of the earth, and we all know dust is very weak. Like mankind today, very, very weak. And Eve was made from Adam's rib. And today, a man and woman are different. One has one more rib in their body. And a man and a woman from that point until today can have children. That's God's plan of marriage, a great plan. Be fruitful and multiply, and we, as humans, got that all wrong. We seldom are fruitful but want to have great sex and multiply.

Thanking you God for Giving Your only Son

We, as a whole, have children before marriage and that's called fornication. We seldom hear that word used today. But that's a sin happening every minute of every day. And the Bible says the wages of sin is death. But we, as human beings, don't seem to read, listen, or even care. I myself am guilty of many, many sins in this life. I had many problems obeying our Father. I am guilty of many sinful acts. But every minute, I'm getting better. For example, if you are blessed to have children, and they are hungry, and you steal a loaf of bread to feed them rather than see them starve to death.

It is called a sin if a person is blessed enough to own a vehicle and is speeding one mile per hour over the speed limit. Is it a sin if a person does not pay his due taxes. Is it a sin if a person is sick and in the hospital and cannot come out to take care of his or her financial affairs? Should they be called a sinner and punished by jail time? And is it a sin to be poor and impoverished? Could and would this happen to any of us? And because we lose our job, are we supposed to lose everything except for our lives? And even sometimes our lives. Should a person be beat or killed because of what they believe or say? So we disagree on many subjects and many things, but is death to another right? War and death, is it always correct? In war, is "I kill or be killed" always correct? Innocent people are involved in most wars. Wars are said to be close to hell. For centuries, wars have waged on. And millions have lost life and limb, and wars are going on right now.

For what reason? I say for greed in many ways. Is sin war? Satan was cast out of heaven as lightning. Was there war in heaven? Cain killed Abel, and man has been killing ever since. It's amazing how man-on-man crimes and sins keep going on.

The Bible makes mention of the people of the earth: the Jews, Ammonite, Horonite, Arabian, Didaites, the Apharsathchites, the Archevites, the Babylonians, the Susanchites, the Dehavites, the Elamites, the Egyptians, the Harorites, the pelkonite, the Tekoite, the anth-toth-ite, the Hushathite, the A-no-hite, the Netophathite, the,

the Pirathonite, the Arbathite, the Shal-bo-nite, the Hararite, the Mecherathite, the Berothite, the Ithrite, the Reubenites, the Mith-nites, the Ash-terath-ites, the Aroerite, the Moabite, the Me-so-ha-lite, the Antothite, the Giblonite, the Gederathite, the Haruphite, the Kor-bites, and the Gadites. This is a few of the people on the earth during Jesus's time on earth. But before I write another word, I must get this point said. God, my Father, you are so close to me. Your love and good-ness so wonderful to me. Your love is so good, it won't let me be. I think about you all the time. You are ingrained in my mind. You are truly the Maker of mankind. I know you took the tears out of my eyes and gave me a whole new beautiful life and new reason to cry tears for you and talk about your miracles happen every minute of every day. That's why you are so loved everywhere. You are God all over the universe, but we as a world can't see it, yet you're my Father, and I love you so dear, and this book I'm writing can't even get close to saying how much I love and treasure you most. It can't express my love for you, but I'll do my best to tell you. I want the world to read and listen what I write and say because I'll be saying this the rest of my days from here on out. I'll always say, Father, let it be as you say. You led me and taught me right from wrong, always giving me a choice to realize. Many times, I was wrong. You did not hurt me that bad, but deep, yes, deep down, I felt bad. I can't blame nothing for my poor choices. It's all a test, and I have to solve them. You taught me to do the right thing in this life you gave to me.

But it took most of my life to feel this much freedom. I've always knew I belong to you, but many of my actions feel far from you. I know many days in my life you had your head down wondering when I would come around, but, Father, you're more than a Father to me. You are my God, and you made me see the true way to go so I'll never ever let you go. As I talk to you, I have to say I'll see you face to face one day, but, Father, I'll need about forty more years on earth to straighten out all my failures. To make much right, that's going to be a big fight. You gave me time to do much in life. Now I'm begging you for more time to get it right. I've never had a lot of nothing because I haven't lived that long, but, Father, please give me more time to change the attitude of wrong to right as I move, and right along, you are the only one who can make that happen for me, so I'm begging you. Please let it happen in your own speed.

This is between you and I, and I know you are the most high, and I'm so proud that you even looke this low to hear me. What I'm saying to you seems very small because you are running an entire universe, wasting time even listening to me. Most judges on earth would think I'm crazy. They don't have time to hear me speak. The whole courtroom would laugh at me. What I have to say means nothing to them anyway, but way up, so very high heavenward, you sit on your throne and lean down low and listen to every word that comes out of my thoughts. You may not say a word, but I know I have been heard, by you, as time goes by, you make your mind what you will do on my behalf. Sometimes I love it and sometimes I say, let it be as my Father says because he's much smarter than I. He gave and still keeps on giving. I read your book, the Holy Bible, the basic instructions, I dont know everything in it, but I'm studying hard. I love listening to you, and I'm greatly inspired by your words. I feel good reading your Word. They give me hope, and I keep on keeping on. I would be more than a waste if I did not get this out of my heart and my mind. I can't keep it in. I have to let it out. It has to be known. My love for you has to be let known throughout the eternal universe. I can't hold it in any longer.

Every minute of every day, you walk with me and talk with me, and you tell me I am your own and, Father, you are my own. I don't own a TV show. I can't talk to millions of people at a time, but I know this book will get out there and will be read by billions of people. Because you are the light of the world, you are my all and all. You are the reason for all season, not only in weather, but in each and every life. You are the difference maker. You are the all in all. You are why we all live. I would love to give all glory to you, and I would love to take this time to thank you for the most meek and loving people I've ever known that you loaned to me ever on earth. I can't thank you enough for the people you put in my life. You made me so very happy. I've come so very far. I've been misunderstood, talked about. I've been robbed, cheated, and scorned, but I just kept moving on. Victory is my goal. And, God, deep in my spirit and soul, doing your will is what I want to do now. Nothing on earth can stop me because your will be done with or without me. I know Satan is around somewhere, but I'm so deep in my Father, I don't have time to worry about him. His time, he knows, is quickly coming to an end. He knows he's been doing wrong for so long. His end is like a sad song. He knows he's been losing for a long, long time, so he's trying to take every one down. He's out there, so don't be fooled by his works. In the end, he will be called the greatest jerk, but let's talk about you and me. Let's talk about this life, some of it that I've experienced. You made it all possible.

Where I lived, I met millions of people. I don't want to call many names because people get angry and think you are playing games, but I met billionaires along the way, baseball players and football players, singers, boxers, preachers, and teachers, just to name a few. But I've never had talks as I've had with you, Father. I think about our talks much of the time now. It's time to write them out loud. I talk to my loving people almost every day. And most of the time, I have little to say. But when I think about the little children around, I can't put thoughts about you down. When I visit a hospital or church, I can't stop praising all the more. And lift you even higher than before. I can only imagine your goodness even more staggering than this little mind of mine. I can't possibly take it all in, but I'm doing my best to spread it to all that will listen. Your greatness is above my explaining, but I'll do my best trying for the rest of my life, trying to tell the world what you have done for me. And

I consider that very personal indeed. You took me out of many sickbeds many, many times and saved my life more times than I can count. I'd woke up in church many a Sunday morning wondering how you got me there. I don't know to this day. I've been to many cities in the world and went the wrong way. There were good streets and bad streets. I had gone down bad streets many times, but in some kind of way, you always turned me around. You sent your angels to get me, and they hurried up and pulled me free. They did not let me be in the wrong place long. They followed your orders to rescue your beloved son. You've protected me from the very start. I know you treasure me deep, yes, deep in your heart, yes. I've had a broken bone or two, but that was all my fault and not yours. I've never killed a soul in my life, and I consider it a miracle the way I ran the streets in all my years. I can't hardly believe it through these tears. I was out and about the streets of the world like the yellow line in the streets all over the place like a telephone pole every day. I was on the road for millions of miles for sure and saw newscast scenes before they were on TV. I mean, way before I was there and gone before the news team arrived. Many, many days go by, and I wonder how I survived. But then I look up high and say, thank you, Father. And keep on working harder and harder every day.

I can't let you forget to praise him as well. Love, honor, and lift him high. He is the reason we all have a life. I was a soldier in the US Army fighting for my life every day. All the way, I was spit on and called all kinds of names. After those experiences, I know I'll never be the same. A black man like me. I thought the world would never let me feel totally free. I got out with an honorable discharge, but deep in my heart, I felt I was marred. But before I end this part, let me be clear. I had just left South Korea and was on my way back to America dressed in my army suit. We landed in the state of California. The people saw me in my uniform and yelled. They spat on me in crowds like I was wrong. They were all angry of course, but I was just doing my job keeping America free. I never speak of this to my family. Doing a job a lot of the time is hard. But that's the way to get it done. I believe in what I do, and I know sometimes I'm loved and sometimes I'm hated, but one day, I'll be graded by my Father in heaven. You watch me all the time, and I'm proud of you for keeping me alive to tell this story to the world. I've been studying your Word, and I know it's the truth, and I hope the world starts to read it too. I've just gotten up and took my shave and my shower and feel really good and refreshed, and I would love to say thank you, Father, for another start to a brand-new start to another lovely day. I realize I'm alive this morning but could be dead this evening. It's all in your hands, but I beg of you. Please let me live. I now realize this is no longer about me, it's all about you. And as your mighty Son, Jesus Christ, said our Father, he was referring to you. Please, Father, let me tell the world of your great deeds that you have done in my short life I've been saved by you. Yes, you gave me a new way of thinking, a new attitude. I dedicate my all and all to you on this day. My life is yours, and I'm more than honored to do so. I hunger for your conversation, your great teaching. You have made my life more than fulfilling. I love writing about your super deeds. I just can't stop praising your name. It's like fire shut up in my bones. This my tests many that I would love to share is more than good, more than giving, more than forgiving, more than faithful, more than righteous, but loving as well. If you never step foot in a church, if you never ever speak to a preacher, a pastor, or any one of God, and by the way, I am not an ordained preacher myself. I don't preach, and I apologize for that, Father, but I do my best to let the world know my Father lives. He still has a throne. He still has a kingdom. He still rules heaven. His territory is my heart. I am his servant. I am his worshiper. He is my king. Soon, and very soon, he will return again, and it's my job to warn you of his return. Our last chance at everlasting life. It's up to me to change your mind. My job to let you know the truth. Even if you live in a cave. If you live all alone, if you live on a rooftop and can't hear or see, if you are on an island and have no contact with anyone, you should know God is God, our only way out, our only heavenly Father, our only way to everlasting life.

Many people say to me that they don't believe. I've talked to people, and they have many reasons. For example, I've heard it said my mother was killed, my dad was killed, my man died, my baby died, and I was so hurt. I was falsely arrested and jailed for years for something I did not do. I've had to struggle all my life. Much harder than you, I've went many a sleepless nights with no food in sight. My people live in poverty. What am I to do? And I always say pray and work hard as you can. God has a way of doing things, and I love the way he does it. All through my life, he has led the way. His truth is still marching on. I was very poor, but I went to school every day. I was ragged and made fun of, but I kept on going. I was talked about as sure as you are born, but I kept on going. I was cold in the winter and hot in the summer, but thanks be to God, I kept on going. I was tired and thirsty, but I kept on going. I studied, and I worked hard, but I kept on going. I rode the bus, and I walked, but I kept on going. I was late a time or two because of bad weather. I was mistreated a time or two. I was misunderstood a time or two, but I kept on going. I was falsely accused a time or two, but I kept on going. I was arrested a time or two, but I kept on going. But this is not about me. It's about our Father who is in heaven. In all I say and do, I know it's a reflection on you. I'm one of your children, and I knew that for a long time and how I know that my past has been fitting as clothes before you for most of my life. Yet I know you still love me and has given me another chance to advance, and I thank you for forgiving me so I can forgive the next person and give them another loving chance in my heart that you've made so dear to you. I want to say thank you, Father, for I have failed you for so many times. I have done way wrong and lot of the time, not right, and all the time I was in your sight. I am only one man, and I have no excuses to give, but please give me the chance to tell the world of your power and goodness so that the world will know of you, and they keep on living. I know you are not secret, you're not under a bush. But I must tell the world about you so they can know why I will always push to let them know who you are and that's why I now live because you are more than the star. My life would not be worth living if not for you, so I'll go to your Holy Bible to tell the people of the world about you. I only have one time to live this life that you gave me, so I want to be remembered by all your people that ever heard of me. I want to spread your Word from earth to heaven and beyond. I love you, Father, and will never stop even after I'm long gone. People will say the man loved God and that conversation will go on and on until you take over in your own time. One day, you will return, and I know that for a fact. And on that day, I hope and pray mankind will be ready. As I am on the day you come back. I used to feel small and unimportant and not very valuable in this world. I called myself Mr. Nobody, and it did not bother me at all. I've never felt that high or mighty because I know this is not about me. I've learned from my mother who always said I don't want to be a big shot or a hothead. She was always quiet and never made a scene. She lived and died polite and honorable.

Righteous and never ever mean to this day, I can never remember my mother being disrespectful to anyone, and Mother has been dead for a while. She taught me right from wrong, but our Father in heaven is where it all began. Deep, yes, deep down in our souls, we all know it's true. Every day of our lives, he is calling on you. I know this song. It's very old, and it's says when love calls you, better answer, and our Father in heaven is calling us all from the rising of the sun till the setting of the sun. He's calling. I'm so glad that I have a church family. I've been a church member of some church for about sixty years. And I thank God for it. I go to honor our Father who lives in heaven. We all know he is real. I make no excuses for what others say or believe. I just pray that they just read God's Word and all his deeds. He living on earth for over thirty-three years and was killed by man. He did not deserve to die, but in his dying, he paid the price for us all. He sacrificed his life for us so that we may live, and I know I can never pay him back for that great thing that he did. He did not want to die, but he gave his life for you and I. Then he went back home to heaven on high. The book of Matthew chapter 5 verse 3–20 states:

> Blessed are the poor in spirit for theirs is the kingdom of Heaven, blessed are they that mourn for they shall be comforted. Blessed are the meek for they shall inherit the Earth. Blessed are they which do hunger and thirst after righteousness for they shall be fulfilled, blessed are the merciful for they shall obtain mercy. Blessed are the pure in heart for they shall see God. Blessed are the peacemakers for they shall be called the children of God, Blessed are they which are persecuted for righteousness' sake for theirs is the kingdom of Heaven, blessed are ye when men shall revive you and persecute you and shall say all manner of evil against you falsely for my sake. Rejoice and be exceedingly glad for great is your reward in Heaven for so persecuted they the prophets which were before you. You are the salt of the Earth but if the salt

have lost his savior where with shall it be salted it is thenceforth good for nothing but to be cast out and to be trodden under foot of men. You are the light of the world a city that is set on a hill cannot be hid. Neither do men light a candle and put it under a bushel but on a candlestick and it given light unto all that are in the house. Let your light so shine before men that they may see your good works and glorify your father which is in Heaven. Think not that I am come to destroy the law or the prophets. I am not come to destroy but to fulfill for verily I say unto you. Till Heaven and Earth pass one jot or one title shall in no wise pass one from the law, till all be fulfilled. Whosoever therefore shall break one of these least commandments and shall· teach men so he shall be called the least in the kingdom of Heaven but whosoever shall do and teach them the same shall be called great in the kingdom of Heaven. For I say unto you that except your righteousness shall exceed the righteousness shall exceed the righteousness of the scribes and Pharisees yet in no case enter in the kingdom of Heaven.

In this thinking, God has made human beings so sensitive that we, as individuals, have things we don't like about ourselves. We seldom think about what is wrong with ourselves. We see what's wrong with our house. We see what's wrong with the government. We see what's wrong with our job. We see what's wrong with our boss. But we seldom see what's wrong with us. It's usually hard to fix ourselves, and the Bible speaks to us on that a lot, and it speaks to the fact that many of us will not see the kingdom of heaven. Because we don't obey, and we don't listen, and most of us have hard hearts. I have many of these faults. I have a problem with forgiving. I have a problem with people who don't like me. But we must learn to love those who hate us. Those who talk about us. Those who steal from us.

Thank You Jesus Christ for Introducing your Father to the World

Those who want to hurt us any way they can. We must learn to be able to learn with every kind of person on earth. We must learn to be able to pass that hard test. It's all a part of living on this earth. It's a very difficult task, but we must be victorious in this battle. We must learn to love those who hate us, and we need prayer to do this. We, as human beings, are made of dust, and dust is very weak from dust we come to dust we shall return so by nature we are spiritually so. We must learn to pray and gain strength to overcome these every-day, every-minute problems. It's test after test. I thank you, heavenly Father, for putting up with me, your son. I'm trying as hard as I can to obey your rules. You said to obey is better than sacrificed, and I believe that, and faith what we truly need and hearing reading his Word, we gain strength. Not physical strength, but spiritual strength. We become victorious by prayer and works, good works for faith without works is dead. I must do something, and praying is always in need. I feel I lack in prayer. I feel I'm weak for lack of prayer. But I'm afraid to say move mountain because I feel it will move and cause death and damage. I know I have a little bit of God's power that he has given me. I know his Word is truth. I know he has use for me. I know he does not need me. I know I can miss out on heaven, but I keep on praying and asking God to keep me, save me, and hold me and my family. I know I need him every hour. Every breath I take, every step I take, I need him, and I tell him so. I'm no preacher that's ordained by man. I don't have a church. Only in my heart and house. I don't own a limousine. I don't own no fancy cars or no airplanes. I don't own no little companies. I'm not a rich man and never has been. My family has no big name, and we are not famously known. But I've never killed anyone, never stolen a thing, never been involved in crime as far as hurting anyone, but then again, I'm wrong. I do crime, I speed in the car sometimes, and that's a crime. I've broken the law. I jaywalked. I spat on the ground before. that's all crime accuses the world. I've committed crimes I did not know were crimes in this life and still don't know if they are crimes or not. I've overeaten. I've more than likely said things by accident that hurt people's feelings, and I apologize for that. I know people are very sensitive more than you will ever know. People are as sensitive as newborn babies. We have many dislikes but very few loves. We hate many things, but hate much more than love. We grew up hating, we usually die hating. Something we, as human beings, are very, very weak. I look inside myself and know I'm in need of spiritual strength. I know I lack a lot of things. I know I need to improve. I know I need growth. I know I need self-help.

Before I go outside and help someone else, I need to help myself. I need to help myself. I need to get myself corrected. I need to help me first. I need to be right, and so far, I'm doing a poor job. I have to correct my own weakness. I'm falling short all the time. I'm in need of much. I find it hard to accept criticism. I find it hard to accept hateful talk directed at me. I find it hard to accept staring and whispering directed at me. I find it hard to be kind to them that tell me they hate me. But I must accept it and thank God, love them and move on. I must learn to love in all cases. It's a hard world, but thanks be to God, I have come to realize it's not about me. It's not about the *I* anymore, it's about our Father who is in heaven. We are supposed to spread his word to all comers of this world and beyond. He is our all and all. We are commanded to do his will, and so far, we are failing miserably. We are not studying his Word. We are not even trying that hard. We know for a fact that one day in some kind of way, we are going to die. We also know that one day that this world will be destroyed by fire. We know that for a fact. We know that our soul and spirit lives forever, and we know that they are us, and we will live somewhere forever, and eternity somewhere, God has some great ideas. For example, our marriage vows are said, I vow to love, honor until death do us part.

Marriage is God's plan and is his idea, a super thought that I love and agree with. Love thy neighbor as thyself, another idea from our Father in heaven. I just love all of his great thoughts and wonderful ideas. I just can't stop praising his beautiful, wonderful name. He brought me into the fold, into the family. I was a Gentile, which is a non-Jew, but I was invited in one day by Jesus Christ, God's beloved son. He was given all power in heaven and earth, and he thought enough of us to bring us into the family—his family. And I would like to say thank you, heavenly Father. In the Holy Bible, John chapter 12 verse 4–6, it says,

> Then sayeth one of his disciples, Judas Iscariot, Simon's son, which should betray him, [said,] Why was not this ointment sold for three hundred pence and given to the poor? This he said, not that he cared for the poor; but because he was a thief, and had the bag, and bare what was put therein.

Telling us all that Judas Iscariot was a thief and don't you know that Jesus knew that all along? It all fits in the masterplan. Each and all of us fits in the plan somewhere.

John chapter 12 verse 26:

> If any man serve me let him follow me and where I am there shall also my servant be if any man serve me, Him will my father honor now is my soul troubled what shall I say father save me from this hour but for this cause came I unto this hour.

Father glorify thy name than came there a voice from Heaven saying I have both glorified it and will glorify it again the people that stood by and heard it said that it was thunder others said an angel spoke to him. Jesus answered and said this voice came not because ofme but for your sakes now is the judgement of this world now shall the prince of this world be cast out and I if I be lifted up from the Earth will draw all men unto me

I read the Bible and draw strength from the word of God. For example, I went to church Sunday, which was yesterday, and there was a young man there, and he came to the front of the church to give his testimony. He told the church that he tried many times to kill himself, and he tried many different ways to commit suicide, and he had a loving, caring family, and they love him dearly. But he went to church, believed in God, but for some reason, he wanted to kill himself. He being a young black man felt lonely. He said he soon became a person who left God and became a nonbeliever. So he went his way, but did not tell his family this. He went out and bought himself a car. He was driving his car, and it ran out of gas, so he got out a gas can and went to get some gas for his car. However, on the way, he sees nine police cars, and one of the police officers tells him to stop. So he stops, then the police officer tells him to show some ID. He reaches for the ID, and he hears all these guns go click.

The police yells, "Don't do that." He yells back, "You said show your ID." This young black man did nothing wrong, but I guess the police were doing their job. But for this young man, he ended up going to the hospital for mental health care. He said the doctors said he had a nervous mental breakdown, so he stayed there for a month or more. His family stayed by his side all through these hard times in his life, but while in the hospital, he stayed in his room all by himself. He felt very lonely. Eventually, the doctor came to him and told him he would release him, which they did. But he felt the same way basically as before. So in his testimony, he said he went to church on this day, and God spoke to him. Our Father who is in heaven is more than good, more than smart, more than caring, more than loving, and more than giving. He's our Father, our Maker, our Creator. More than our all and all, he sees all and knows all. The young man told his story to the church, and it was one of the most interesting I've ever heard. God has stood by me in every way. I have this book as my testimony to our Father in heaven. And I'll do my best to lift him up to the very best of my ability because my best is as filthy as a rag before him, but I'll do my best to say thank you, my loving, caring Father. I'll start by saying thank you, Father, and fellow human beings. I would like to thank you for reading my story. Our Father keeps us alive every day. He's by our side every second of every day. He gives us choices to do what we want. But it's our job to find our Father who is in heaven. I've been trying but not my best to tell every man, woman, and child who our Father is. Jehovah God and his loving Son Jesus Christ are the ones we look to, the ones we pray to, the Father who is in heaven, and know for sure that Satan is in hell. I have decided to serve our Father in heaven the rest of my life. I've decided to serve our Father who is in heaven the rest of my life. I've decided to testify to the entire world that I will do my best to obey our Father's will and write these things in a book. In the book of John chapter 21 verse 25, it says and there are also many other things which Jesus did which if they should be written, everyone, I supposed that even the world itself, could not contain the books that should be written, amen. That tells me we don't give Jesus Christ enough credit for his wonderful works representing our Father He did great and wonderful works that are ignored by us all as people. I know it's my job to tell the whole world this before I die. I have to get it out to the people with my all and all. I feel I've got to do this with everything within me personally. It's his command to me, and I love it. I feel so good doing my Father's will as Jesus said, not my will but your will be done. I hear him speaking to me. In fact Psalms 145 verse 18–21 says,

> The Lord is high unto all them that call upon him to all that call upon him in truth. He will fulfill the desires of them that fear him: he also will hear their cry and will save them. The Lord preserveth all them that love him: but all the wicked will he destroy. My mouth shall speak the praise of the Lord: and let all flesh bless his holy name forever and ever.

I am made humble by our Father. He is my Savior. He is my God. He makes me humble in prayer. He makes me humble in life. Every day I see his wonderful works. It's a great thing to see him keep me alive. It's a blessing to see his word come true each and every day of my life, to see his great protection over a family big and small. To see him answer prayer every minute of every day. To see his untold mercies in effort. To see him still on the throne, decisions, still in action, him working on our behalf every second of every day. Answering my prayers every day. All day long taking care of me from the rising of the sun until the setting of the same I love the way you protect my family that you loaned to me for a little while. How you feed and clothe them. How you give them food and water every day of their lives. How you give them a choice to worship you if they choose to, but you don't force yourself on anyone. How you keep the ungodly yet alive like myself like me. I did not deserve a Father like you. You are everyone's Father, but the world does not know that yet. They don't know who you are yet. They don't respect and understand yet. They don't love and honor you like they should yet. I thank you for putting up with me, your child that loves and honors you and prays to you and begs for your mercy for a world of people. Please, Father, have mercy on the world. Please forgive us in Jesus Christ's holy name. Lord, I beg you to give the people of the world of the universe another chance to get it right. Lord, let me have a chance to warn them of the dangers of hell and the eternal flames of hell. Father, let me warn mankind. Please give the human race more time to correct itself. I've made up my mind to do my best to do your will to the best of my ability, and I feel I'm falling well short of my own goals. Give me more strength, more knowledge to help do your will. I need more of your power to write more of you to help me do your will for church and for mankind. Lord, help me to let mankind know you are the only hope ever. I live a life of love because of you. My family eats well because of you. My family knows you but not well because of me. I go to church worship, thanks to you. We live in a house, thanks to you. We own a vehicle, thanks to you, at least us on the bank. We don't own many things, but we are grateful unto you for what we do have. I know one in five people across the world go to bed hungry every night. I know fire destroys homes and families every day. I know homes are broken into every day, and people are robbed and killed every day. I know floods and rain destroy towns and villages on a regular basis. Hurricanes are all over the world and destroy every day, yet our Father is still protecting all day, every day. He is still on that throne. He is my Father in whom I am well pleased with him. I love my Father. He may not be your God, but he is your Father. Your heavenly Father and Jesus told us that he said our Father which art in heaven. Our Father in the book of Isaiah 54 chapter 17, it says:

> No weapon that is formed against thee shall prosper; and every tongue that shall rise against thee in judgment thou shalt condemn. This is the heritage of the servants of the Lord, and their righteousness is of me, saith the Lord.

Also, it is written, let the wicked forsake his way and the unrighteous man his thoughts and let him return unto the Lord, and he will have mercy upon him and to our God for he will abundantly pardon. And Isaiah chapter 55 verse 11: "So shall my word be that goeth forth out of my mouth: it shall not return unto me void." And, Father, I want to thank you for your grace and abundant mercy. Thank you for opening up your heaven's gift that you are showering down on me. Thank you for gifts I know I don't deserve. But your grace, your giving, your wisdom has saved, sanctified me. Showering your love down on me if not for you. I can't help myself without you. I can't help others without you. I am lost. Without you, I am without anything. I want the world to know that we, as people, have only one life to get this correct. Please get this right. Jesus, the son of God, came from heaven to get us to do God's will. He said not my will but your will be done. The righteous will of our father. No more killing, no more beatings, no more stealing, no more raping. The wrongdoing must stop in every way that we, as people, do our wrong. Please, I beg of you. Read the right thing and do it. We, as people, only have earth to live on and heaven and hell when we die. I am one who got it the hard way. I went to school, and I am not a simple man. I am not a common man. I am well educated. I've got a degree or two to my name. I've worked a job and went to school at the same time for years. After that, I've worked two jobs most of my life, and I raised my children and did my very best and helped many others to raise theirs. I feel I am saved and sanctified and covered by the blood of Jesus Christ. I am healed by him. I know I should and could have been dead a long time ago, but he has given me time to warn you of his return. He will be returning soon, and through his kindness and everlasting care and love that knows no bounds, he has given me the right to tell you to change your way, do his will, or surely die. Sin equals death, and death through sin is hell and that's an eternal sentence. A life that never ends of hurt and pain. It is written in the Holy Bible. I call it basic instructions before leaving earth. I beg all people. Please, I beg, cry, and pray to God to turn you around, but in the end, it's all up to you to do and believe and have faith in our Father in heaven. The one and only Jehovah God, his Son, Jesus died for us. He and his Father now lives in heaven. I am not a pastor of any church but of my own house. The fact of the matter is, I am not a preacher of any. Note I don't own or run any business of any kind. I don't have any kind of following. I don't lead any group and don't have much in the way financially or money. As people would say my name is J. L. McLaurin, I refer to myself as Mr. Nobody. But a son of God who is my all and all, literally my all and all, and if you don't know, now you know yours too. He is my Father, my leader, my counselor. I've been in a jail cell for little of nothing. I've been on street corners. I've been in alleyways. I've been on many, many jobs. I've been in many people's homes including my own. I've been with many different groups of people, family, and friends' picnics and parties. And on my vacations, trips, walks, runs, drives, ride fairs, and many church affairs, I would love to say God has always had his loving angels there for me. I always know he had his angels in the crowd for me, and I will go on to say for us, his beloved, every day, all of this way, he is protecting his people. I am one of his protected. I have things to tell the world. It's like fire shut up in my bones. There is a time for everything, and my time to tell you is now. I get my inspiration from our Father who is in heaven and people gone on to be with him, but I know of others that have wrote a book or two.

Thank You Jesus for All Your Giving!

I've read a book by a writer. The name of the book is the Bible. As history, the writer was a rich man and did not believe the Bible. So he set out to see if there was any truth to this Holy Bible. He spent a lot of money checking this out. After reading and much work and much investigating, he has found out the same thing that I know. That everything in the Holy Bible is true. I got in a conversation with my doctor. We were talking about Gentiles. What is a Gentile? I know a Gentile is not a Jewish person, but he says a Gentile is a nonbeliever, which I believe is also true. I know Jesus Christ let us all into God's kingdom. I know some of my people were slaves in Egypt. I know many of my people were slaves in America. If you see I am a man of color. I have studied the Bible a little. I've read a little and have pondered his word a lot. I have lived a little and have been through a lot. I've worked a lot and earned a fair pension, but I am not satisfied with my performance unto my Father in heaven. I know I must do better with the time he has given me. My dad, Lencola McLaurin, told me to please don't write anything until he died. The man died over ten years ago, and now is my time to write about our more than great and loving Father. I don't feel any pressure. I just want to do his will and get it right for all of mankind. I feel like this in my heart, soul, and mind. Never lose heart, so even until this day, I still pray hard every day and talk to my Father in heaven all along my hard day. All along the road, I'm thanking him for the opportunity to give him the praise to have fun in doing what I'm doing today. He's given us a chance to do great things today and allowed me to do a job that he's letting me do in his great way. I'm so proud of my Father who is so strong. He lets me keep on moving along. He keeps an eye on me and even watches me while I sleep. Even if I should die while I sleep. He's even in control. Even then, he has my soul to keep. I only live a little while, but I am going to give him much grace, love, and pride. I'm working every day to let him know I love him, and what he's doing every day I'll never forget. He's still on his throne. He's never left me all alone. He's been with me every step of the way, and I'm sure he has carried me more than half that way. He keeps me alive, I am sure. He sends his angels back and forth from heaven to earth for more than a tour. They are looking and checking on my Father's behalf and doing a great job. I know my best will never be good enough, but I'll do my best to let it be known while I was yet alive, Lord God, that I gave it my best shot. I told all the people about you. I told them all about your truth. I told them all how good you were to me and how you even gave me a family. How you feed me every day. How you kept a roof over my head. How you told me right from wrong. How you protected me all my life. How you gave me health and strength. How you gave me a job, a house to live in a church to praise you, a will to love even when things weren't going my way. You still would give me a soft pillow to lie on when I cry. You would dry my tears and lift me up and even in my low, low spirit, I felt bad many a days, but you would change that spirit in many different ways. I would cry deep down inside, but you, in your deep wisdom, would send another soul, not to take their place, but to keep us aware of your great control. You put another smile on our face and let us know you are still the greatest. The one and only

God, and that's the fact, the truth, the God forever and ever more. You got a way of doing things, and I love the way you do it. You add and take away. Every day, you make change all along the way. We, as people, hardly even notice what's going on. You bring rain, sun, and storms. You bring darkness, light, and even day. You make hot and cold, and you bring changes throughout the day. Every day is different. You make it that way. I find it interesting the way you go about your work. You make it dark, you call it night, yet in heaven, there is not night. You made earth your footstool, and it's so close to your heart. We, as people, are so far apart. We seldom talk to you, and I am guilty of not talking to strangers even to this day, but I have to change that thought in order to spread your ways. Your laws must be heard in order to be observed. It's my job to let your word be heard, and it's up to me to get it out there to the people of our world. I've been quiet for much too long now. It's time to put your word out there strong. I'm writing books to let the world know it's always been your time and world. It's time to go.

A great example of God's warning is Ezekiel 3:17–21. It says:

Son of man I have made thee a watchman unto the house of Israel: therefore hear the word at my mouth, and give them warning from me. When I say unto the wicked, Thou shall surely die; and thou givest him not warning, nor speakest to warn the wicked from his wicked way, to save his life; the same wicked man shall die in his iniquity ... but thou hast delivered thy soul. Again, When a righteous man doth turn from his righteousness, and commit iniquity, and I lay a stumbling-block before him, he shall die: because thou hast not given him warning, he shall die in his sin, and his righteousness which he hath done shall not be remembered; but his blood will I require at thine hand. Nevertheless if thou warn the righteous man, that the righteous sin not, and he doth not sin, he shall surely live, because he is warned; also thou hast delivered thou soul.

So please warn people to stop doing their evil deeds. Stop sinning because the works of sin is death. Pray without sin, pray for the good of mankind. In the book of Ezekiel chapter 5 verse 8:

> Therefore thus saith the Lord God; Behold, I, even I, am against thee, and will execute judgments in the midst of thee in the sight of the nations. And I will do in thee that which I have not done, and whereunto I will not do any more the like, because of all thine abominations. Therefore the fathers shall eat the sons in the midst of thee, and the sons shall eat their fathers; and I will execute judgments in thee, and the whole remnant of thee will I scatter into all the winds.

I pray that our Father in heaven has pity on us, his children. I pray for every human being that our God has mercy on us. I remember being in the US Army about forty years ago. I was in basic training early in the morning. Before I went to sleep, I was in a huge barrack or long army living quarters, and I whispered a prayer. It goes: now I lay me down to sleep, I pray to God my soul to keep. All of a sudden, it seemed like almost every soldier in there were saying that same prayer to this day. I am shocked. People know who God is, but they try to keep it to themselves, but I want the people to help me let the world know about our great Father who lives in heaven. I can't get enough of praising his name. I just love lifting him up each and every day and in every single way. I was in the US Army and in God's army at the same time. I'm in God's army forever more, and I am so grateful to be one of his many servants. And I love it all day, every day. I personally find myself having many debates with people of other faiths. And people with other beliefs, they believe in other gods. I speak with people of the Muslim world. Others who believe in Buddha. I believe in Jehovah God, the Father of Jesus Christ. The first of the dead to come back alive. I recall years ago when I was in the US Army. I lived all over South Korea, and we lived under martial law, and what that means is you had to be off the streets of South Korea from twelve at night until five in the morning. You had to be inside a building, or you could be shot down by the military forces doing their jobs, and they did an excellent job. All the while I was there, the people were scared to be outside the house because many had been killed and many arrested. It was frightening to live under martial law. I watched the army enforce their laws to the best of their ability, and I say they did a super job. They killed people, even soldiers that I knew personally. It was a hard, harsh law controlled by hard, harsh people. But I loved all the people of Korea. I've never seen a more loving people, and I used to go on service tours. They were so beautiful and rich. I used to cry like a newborn baby, and I still remember the beauty only God can give, show, and share to us as human beings. I'll never forget his kindness that I saw with my own eyes. It will last an eternity. God is so sharing, caring, merciful, giving, and obeying our lives, our hearts, our minds, and our spirits to his wonders of everyday life. What a blessing to see him work his miracles every single day all over the world. Everywhere around the globe. It is truly a rich thing to see our Father working from his throne to people's hearts and minds. He is more than great, he is my all and all, and I want the world and the universe to know I just can't stop praising his name. I refuse to stop worshipping him. Can't stop telling of his goodness to me. How he rescued me from a hardworking solider in the US Army to a soldier of his own making. How he has led me from combat zone to combat zone, and yet he has kept me alive. From death's door to the church's door, from hospital bed to the prayer at the foot of the bed, from the war-torn country to the world of the USA, from crying tears of hurt, pain, and tears to tears of joy with family and people that call themselves friends back to loved ones. A Deliverer, a Maker, a Creator, a living, loving God who does not ever make a mistake. Who always gets it right. And in the end, we, as humans, will see he is always right and never ever wrong. For he is our God, our Father, our all and all. Worthy to be praised at all times. We are just not as smart as he is. He gives, and he takes away. Blessed be his holy name. We cannot outthink our Father. His thoughts are much higher than ours. His power much greater, and his love much stronger than ours. He controls much, much more. He's literally running a universe every single day with but a day off. I would love to thank our Father for one of his great greatest gift known to man. The gift of life. Then I would love to thank him for the great gift of prayer. The ability to speak out loud. The ability to think in silence, and he yet hears me to be able to understand my laugh and my cry. My every feeling by and by. He knows my every thought. He's even aware of my walk. He can't be tricked or deceived, not even by me. He's always around. Always near even when I can't see my way clear. He's more than my Father, more than my God. He's much, much more. He's my all and all. When I'm sick, lying in bed, he has his angels adjusting my head. His angels are alive and well. They even protect me in a jail cell. He's my Father, but much, much more. He works his job every day and does such a great job. We, as people, seldom give him credit for such great work done from before the beginning of time. His love out-lives anything in any human's mind. He's been on his throne for so very long. I give my Father praise and love all day long. I know he always busy running his universe, but he even has time for me. And that makes me feel high in this earth. I have not done anything of note to deserve his great Bible quotes. But one thing I know for sure, he's my Father, and I love him more than dear. I can truly say I can only speak for myself. He's my all and all, and nothing else can take his place on my deathbed or where I die. Nothing known to man will equal the love, pride, Father dear. Let me make perfectly clear. That's why I wrote this book to say my God,

Father, Jehovah, can never be replaced. Every day that I wake up, I'm in debt to him, and I know I can never repay what he did. Every day, I go forth and say, thank you, Lord, and thank you for hearing my lifelong calls. I know I've never deserved you and all that you do for me every step of the way. Your favor, your gifts, along life's hard highway, but I keep pressing forward all day long, and you keep giving me strength to keep going on. I know one day, but it won't be soon, you will make room for me in your great upper room. I'm not looking for death anytime soon, but I want another sixty years of life before I give up the ghost before being called to my room. You know I'm out here tough, hard, and strong doing my very best. I feel like I'm bearing down doing better and better every day to do what you want your will has to say, because your will be done in heaven and earth, and I'm making it happen for sure while on earth. Because in heaven, my job will be done, so give me more time down here. To get the job done. Down here is hard, tough, and mean, but you've given me the skills and all the equipment I need to make your will be done. Give me the time to make a hard, hard run. A run at change, a run for your will to be done on every street corner and in every alley in the world.

Give me more time to give it a turn, a chance to make right with all my might. I know my family's up in heaven looking at me. I know there's talk about what I'm going to do. Is he going to be true to you or is he going to fade away and be all talk like others and that's all he ever will? And even if he gets here, what does he have to say? Can he say he helped the human race in any way? Did he change anyone's life along the way? Did he do anything right while he was there? Is the earth different? Is there any change? Are people still walking around in chains? Is there still jail rapes and killings? Is there still hurt feelings? Is there still stealing? Is there still wars and riots every day? Are people still hungry and homeless all along the world's highways? Is there people dying because they are hungry? Is there still people being robbed? Or children seeking mothers who have no man to help raise their beloved babies? Are people still being shamed because of this or that even their name Is there still crime committed every day?

We all see we have a long, long way to go, so let's put heaven deep in our hearts and minds and make earth a much better place. We must do it. We all must try and do much more before we die. Life is not promised to no one. Every day, we are maybe under the gun. There are so many ways to die. We all get the chance so day so how On the radio or on the TV, we see death, destruction, and hurting people all around the world. Death is certain and that's a fact. Once we leave here, there is no coming back. We only have two places we can go, and please be sure you are on the way to God's place. The God who made it all. The one who keeps it all in place. I had a talk the other day. He made me feel so good in so many ways. He asked me hard questions from his heart questions that hurt me deep to my soul, spirit, and heart. He said to me, one day soon, you will be going home with me. Heaven will be your home for eternity and that's forever, my child. You will see everyone there and talk forever. They will ask you all kinds of questions for sure you will be in the middle of heavenly hosts. They will say there is much crime below: rapes, robberies, heartache, and killings, for sure. There is so much sin going on, and while you were there, did you stop anything? Because you were on earth a long time. Did you stop any wars or riots? Did you stop a neighborhood from dying? Did you feed a hungry nation down there? Did you free a single slave? Did you ignore the people in need? Did you administer to the people's needs? Were you rich or poor? Did you speak for the children that had great needs? Or were you one in great need? Were you a prisoner locked away in jail? Or were you a crime fighter somewhere? Did you preach in some church or did you stay home and look at the people suffer? Did you do your very best? Do the people remember any of your work? You just got to heaven, and we've been here a long time, so while you are here, let's talk about it? Yes, I'm still on earth, and these are four questions asked of me. I have to do much better in life to answer these hard questions of me. But, in fact, they're very easy. I have to do much, much better. More than ever, I feel tears going down my face. I feel shame and disgrace. I just don't feel good at all. So far in life, I feel appalled. I'll have to do better by mankind. So far, I'm failing by even my standards. I'm way behind, so I say, Father in heaven, give me much more time to kill sin in every way I can and do my best to break the long cycle of murder in human beings' lives. The killing of newborn babies, what a super crime. We, as humans, have a long, long way to go. Father in heaven, please help us to go forth in your righteous way. Every single second of every day. Father, man has so many laws that I break every day from speeding the vehicle to jaywalking to spitting on the ground. All along the way to hurting people's feelings that I don't even know about to for-getting all kinds of occasions that slipped my mind. And I feel bad because I'm filled with so much love from above. I have so many things going on. I have to have help from above to keep it all going. I have a wife and children and much family that God gave to me. I'm more than thankful to him for his much giving. So as you see, I'm not ready for heaven yet. I have much more work to get done here on earth. I'm generations behind my Father's will. I'm so far behind that I feel a cold, cold chill. I must catch up and improve my job. I'm ashamed of my weak job so far, but I promise to do better as I go along, for in my Father, I am strong. So it's up to me to do a better job because he is giving me more time, and I know I'm only flesh and blood. But I came from the strength of our Father from above. So it's up to me to give my all and all because man needs much help to keep on going and, Father, I am so grateful to you for introducing me to you during this life at an early age, and I know my very best is a filthy rag before you. But I want you to know I'll keep on putting these filthy rag before you with my all and all intended.

Well, Lord, today I've decided to go to the library and check out some books. I've been a heavy reader my entire life, and I love learning things. However, you are the master teacher. I feel the more I know, the more I need to know. This life is so full. There're so many things to do in this life. Father, I would like to say thank you. I feel you are the Creator of love. I feel so much love from my family. I go to North Carolina, and I feel so much love from my beloved family. I feel the glow of heat. I feel the love so much that I see the tears and feel my own tears flowing down my face. That is pure love from our God up above. They are not rich people or very well-off. But they have the love of our God built into their lives. They teach and live God's rules and laws and tell others all about what he has done in our lives. I cry when I think about the miracles God has done. Miracles every day to each and every one of us. I pray and thank God for his love and favors, and I love his wonderful loving favors. I pray for all of my family all over the world, and even the ones that don't even know me. I am a man of color, and most of my family knows, but some of my cousins are blonde-haired and blue eyes, and they don't even know me. But they are blood family and family from years ago.

God made that all so. God has a way of doing things, and I just love how he does it. People are all

God's children, but a lot don't know how much love he has for them. We all have to seek him because he seeks us out all day every day. He's calling our spirit. Our father is calling us all. Please read his Holy Word. We only get this one life on this earth. Only one chance. So let's make the best of it. People live all kinds of lives. No two people are the same and never have been, but our Father is so good, kind, and merciful. He made everyone different and said, love thy God with all thy heart, soul, and mind. God is first in every way in my life. I'm speaking for myself. I was visiting a church with my own. Church and that church's pastor was celebrating twenty years of service for the wife and pastor. Well, in this wonderful service, one of our ministers spoke about the Holy Ghost. He said that he has the love of the Holy Ghost. Let me explain the love of the Holy Ghost to the best of my ability. Jesus Christ is his Father's Son. His father is Jehovah God. Psalms 18:7, it says that men may know that thou whose name alone is Jehovah art the most high over all the earth. So when Jesus Christ was here on earth, he knew he would be killed on the tree. So he let it be known that he would leave behind the Holy Ghost for all mankind. Because he said (being Jesus Christ), speaking all power in heaven and earth is given unto me by my father Jehovah God, and I want the reader to seek that in the holy Bible because as sure as God is alive, so is that word. I go to praise God everywhere I go. I go to lift his holy name, and that's every place I go. I'm sold on the word of our father and that will never change. So my job from this day forth is to convince you. And that's one of the many reasons I love writing these wonderful books I love doing what I do and praising my Father in heaven. I just can't get enough of it. I want to give respect to the people of Buffalo, New York, and all the people of New York City, and I would love to thank my church family. I have a huge church membership, thanks be to our God. I went to our church yesterday and listened to the wonderful services involved. It's truly well thought out because God is in charge. He tells us mankind to follow his Word and his leadership. And I love the way God does things in his own way, in his own time. I love how he alone speaks to me. How he coddles me. How he shows me things in a way only he can. How he teaches me as only he can. He is closer to me than my own heartbeat. Closer than the blood that runs warm in my veins. Closer than the love I have for myself. I speak for myself and just can't stop praising his name. And I must keep on telling this beautiful story of our Father who truly does live in heaven. I'm just getting started by the way. Just in case you forgot, my name is Jimmy L. McLaurin out of Pine Hurst, North Carolina. But now I live outside of Buffalo, New York, a small town to many. Most people see Buffalo, New York, as a small poor town, and that's about the true case. But in Buffalo, I've learned a lot about life's long, hard road. This life is a life of work. It's a life of experiences. It's a life of hurt and pain. It's a life of schools, learning, and jobs. It's a life of people from around the world. It's all about right and wrong, weak and strong, sin and the wages of sin. The works of sin is death, and the gift of God is eternal life. And that is a wonderful gift, my people, as I think about it. I was near the University of Buffalo last week, and there used to be two stores that sold Bibles on Main Street, but over the years, they both closed their doors and shut down. And, as of now, I see the closing of many Bible stores in America, and it's sad to say that seems to be a trend in our neighborhoods. All over the United States of America, we have to be very careful. Because as of yet, I have not mentioned it, but we, as human beings, have a natural enemy, and it's Satan. The evil one. He does exist. He is here on our earth, make no mistake about it. He is here to kill, maim, and destroy. Remember to keep that somewhere in your minds. Because right about now, Satan knows his time is very short. He knows it's almost over for him. He knows his end is very near.

Without You There is No Family

Even death, time is almost up soon and sooner than you would think. Our Father is planning his sudden and quick return. It will be so fast. It will be sudden. God is planning his return. It will be very soon, and I beg of you, world, to get it right before he returns. Please make up your minds to do his will. Sacrifice is not as good as obedience. Obey his word. I am struggling to get it right. I am committed to do my Father's will regardless of what it takes from me personally. He allows me to live, and I am most gracious to him for his mercy that I can't explain my appreciation enough. I know every day he has his arms stretched out to us from the rising of the sun until the setting of the same, and I am more than grateful. I know life and death is in the tongue. I know he can kill, and he can make alive, and none can deliver from his hand, and I know that's to be true. My personal experience are many. Over the years, I served in the US Army, and I know I should have been dead many times over and over again. I witnessed people being shot and called accidents that I feel were not accidents. I've seen people pull guns on me personally and pull the trigger, and the gun jammed. And this has happened more than once. I lived in a country under martial law. For over a year, the people were close to terrified. You had to be inside a house, home, or hotel after twelve o'clock. If you were on the streets, the military could and would gun you down. You must thank God that, so far, the United States is not totally under martial law. But I thank our Father in heaven for his so many loving blessings. The people he has put in our lives. Our loving children, our loving mothers and dads, our loving brother and sister, our aunts and uncles, our cousins and friends that are closer than family. Some of us don't have much family, and I've heard of people that don't know any of their own family. And I've heard of people who now spend their entire lives in the beds of hospitals or at home. I've heard of people that are bedridden and housebound, and that's not much talked about in today's world. I feel that Christ's way of life is being attacked all over the world. I feel that right is held up by God's might, and right is God's will, and I truly believe that faith without work is dead. A person must have faith, but I believe you must put that faith to work by some kind of work no matter how small we may deem it to be. Work on your dreams and never stop doing your job. And make sure it's not the wages of sin. Because the wages of sin is death. Every day, I try to remember to thank my Father for another day of life. I know I don't deserve it, but I pray and ask for his loving mercy every day. I know it's all him that keeps the world alive, and I'm sure of that. As sure as I live, I know it's because of my Father in heaven. He has shown himself more than right, more than just, more than merciful, more than strong, more than righteous, more than forgiving, more than a Father, and truly more than I can ever say, but truly much, much more, but truly my Father, my God, and I can never say enough to thank my God. So I'll keep on praising forever and ever in this humbly written book that he inspired me to write in his most deserved right. I just can't stop praising his name. Thank God for Jesus Christ, the first of the dead, as he said, I am proud of my Son, and I am proud of our Father who truly does live in heaven. Every day that I live, he becomes more real in my life. As a matter of fact, I would like to say I believe there are only three types of beings in our infinite number of universes. They are human beings, the angel who travels back and forth from heaven to earth by assignment, which are in the same class as we call sometimes aliens, same as angels, and our Father's most elite. He probably has many, many more that I'm not aware of. But I do know that these three are on my map, and they can travel anywhere at his whelm, and he does have them traveling for our regard. On a regular basis, he's daily working on our behalf around the clock. He is running the universe, some more attention more than others. Because man needs much more attention than most. We are able to destroy this world, and without his loving help, we would have destroyed it already, but through prayer and his mercy, we still live on, and I am indebted to him all the more. I just can't stop praising his name. I just won't stop praising his name. We, as people of the earth, must at some point and time realize who he is and what he is doing in our behalf. He is getting closer and closer to returning, and when he does, our time will be up. No more time for forgiveness. No more time to get sin out of our lives. No more time to make a personal choice between right and wrong. We, as human beings, will be judged, and our lives will be put in the balance. Will we be one of his children or not? Will he say yes or no to our short-lived lives? Did we pass or will we fail our task? That he put before us? I know this to be a hard life, and so much harder for some than others. The majority of us have more problems, more sickness, more bills, less money, less or more family, less or more friends, more things that go wrong, but please remember, our Father sits high but always looks low. He is always on our side. He has never left us. We have left him. He has never quit his job of running his universe and never will. He has never forsaken us and never will. He is our all and all, and I beg of you. Please believe that. I am so thankful that you have humbled me in this life and let me know I'm like a blade of grass in this world. I came to be born and die. I came with nothing and will leave with nothing. And I am more than proud to be one of you. Many beloved children and I would love to say you are my beloved Father in whom I am well pleased. I just can't stop praising your name. It will never run out of style. I'll never get tired of saying it. I'll always do my best to get better at doing your marvelous will. I am not doing a good-enough job even now. I'm below your standards, and I know I am, but, Lord, I will do much,

much better. I beg of you. Please give me more of you in every way.

I earlier spoke of God's elite I believe he has beings capable of going to the sun and getting power from the sun that will last for millions of years and powers that mankind at this time can only dream about in the Bible. It is said in my Father's house are many mansions, and if it were not so, I would have told you this age is called the age of knowledge. Yet we, as mankind, know so little about the most important things in our lives. Our heavenly Father is the number 1 thing in our lives, yet we act as though it's a big secret. Like it's hidden under a bush. Like we don't know God exists. Like we are totally in the dark, and that's another point I would love to share with you. There is no darkness in heaven. I've heard it said before that only 140,000 beings will live in heaven and that the earth will be made all new. But even if that will be true, you, as God's children, will be able to visit heaven as often as you would like. I believe earth and heaven will be almost the same as we, as people, were invited unto God's family by the loving Jesus Christ one day. He said our Father, which is in heaven, hollow be thy name. Thy kingdom come. Thy will be done on earth as it is in heaven. Give us this day our daily bread. So much is said in these few words. Jesus gave us the privilege to be part of the heavenly family. He literally put us, as all human beings, in his holy family, and he said all power in heaven and earth is given unto me, and he used much of his power in our behalf. He has drawn me unto him. He has let me know of his great love. He has taught me. He is speaking to me when all seems to be quiet. He has changed my mind, my way of thinking. He has turned my hate to love. My hard heart to one of understanding. My tongue from evil speaking to one of much more love, but every day I'm getting better. I'm not where I want to be, but slowly but surely, I'm getting there. This is not about me. This is about our Father in heaven. He is giving me the chance to glorify him and his loving Son before his grand return, and I appreciate him for this chance to raise him unto all mankind. When he returns, it will be too late. So let us celebrate our more than great God. Let us celebrate. I am a miracle for his changes he did to me. He changed my heart, my soul, my spirit, and my mind. It took time, but he changed even my terrible mind. I thought I was mistreated and hated, forsaken, shortchanged in many transactions, and the truth of the matter is, I may have been. But the love of our God has shown me I am not the headlines in his universe. He is the reason for so great a season in our lives. We are so far a weak people. We came from dust, and to dust we shall return. Our Father is the one that should be first in our minds when we wake up early in the morning until we close our eyes at night. He should be first and foremost in our lives, hearts, and minds.

One of my major goals in life is to live at least 120 years in this lifetime, and I believe that is a reasonable request. I feel that 120 years will give me time to complete most, if not all of which is required of me in this lifetime. I got into a conversation with a homeless man. He told me that his house had burned down, and he was forced to move into a homeless shelter. He was still in love with our Father in heaven. He is still very grateful and appreciates the fact he still lives. He lost much in life, but he feels he gained much. He realizes who our Lord is. He spoke to me about the rewards that came to him through this loss. But he got great gains along the way. The man actually surprised me with his faith, trust, loyalty, honor, and much love. And I believe the man was very poor, money wise, but rich in righteousness. He is one in a million, and the man was in his late twenties or early thirties. He is very well read on God's Word, which I think is wonderful. He spoke of Jesus Christ and our Father who is in heaven. The wonders, the might of our Lord is so great, and I am so glad that the Word is getting out there. I'm not out in the streets much, but when I am, I love telling them. Not pressuring anyone, not bullying anyone, not being overbearing, but humbly with grace and much love. I know for a fact that much of the world's people will want to kill me and anyone else that says they believe in Jesus Christ's teachings. I know I would be beheaded, killed at the least. And I know death is the order of the day. For many people who preach God's Word, I am a believer of Jesus Christ. I've never been a preacher ordained by any state government. I've never had a church or a congregation. I've never been more than a junior deacon. In any church, I've never had any power. As a church leader, I've never led much more than a choir leader. But I believe I am a son of God. I have much faith, and I still put in work, but I am not in the power physically to do what I would love to do. I've never went door to door. But I know people that do. I love God as much as they do, but my calling is through writing and telling you through speaking through books. I'm not rich. I don't own any radio stations. I don't own any TV stations. I don't own any huge speaking halls or have the money for any big stages to speak to the world, but I'm getting it done. I don't have a huge following as of yet, because, as of yet, not much more than my church family knows my agenda. Most people I know don't know the deed seeded feelings in my heart, soul, and mind. I'm sure they would not be surprised at my feelings for our Father in heaven. But before I introduce this chapter, I feel very sad. I am going to talk about the term *ethnic cleansing*, the killing of man on man, women killing women. It is truly very sad to me. The fact that Cain killed Abel and killing is still going on today. It hurts me down to my bone marrow. I just feel we, as people, can and should do a better job. We can do a much better job saving each other's lives. Killing people is a terrible thing. Man's lives are short enough as it is, and when you think about it, the setting of the sun of our lives is very quick. I mean, our death is the setting of the suns in this life. Jesus wept for all mankind and so do I. The Romans killed the Greeks, the China man killed the Africans, Asians killed Asians, the Jews killed the Jews, and all of them killed each other. It is called ethnic cleansing by many, and they kill each other for a million different reasons. Even how they smell, the color of one's eyes, the way one talks, the way their skin color is, how they pray, and whom they pray to. Whom they love or whom they don't love. The food they love or don't. Like the thought of respect or disrespect. The fighting and killing over land to this day all over the globe.

Israel is a great example. Since Jesus Christ has been here, the Jews have been at war with the Palestinians, and to this day, they are still at it. Japan had wars with China. France and England had wars. Germany fought the United States. England and the colonies had wars. The world has more wars than I know about. And it has been said before I was born that war is hell. I believe that, at one time, there was war even in heaven. But I don't believe that genocide ever took place in heaven, but on earth, we have many dark-minded people who do dark-hearted things, and many people in group take part of genocide. People are killed because of who they are. A race of people usually are destroyed because of whatever you can name, almost any reason, and people will kill for whatever, and that's the human race. They literally kill for no reason. Most of the time, it's a reason that could have been solved without wars, deaths, murders, and the savage acts of mankind. And when you think about it, people kill over food. They have been known to eat each other. People have fought and died over water. Millions of people have died over religious beliefs, arguing who's right and who's wrong. I have heard it said that the word of the Muslims will be spread by the tongue or by the sword, and that is true to this day. I know for a fact if a Japanese warrior pulls his sword before he puts it away, he must draw blood, so he will cut himself before he puts it away. Death is taught by almost every culture and nation all over the globe. I witnessed it in my lifetime in many places. I've personally been a US solider and in the US Army. The basic training you are taught is self-defense, which is training to kill point-blank. You are taught to protect yourself to defend the USA, and that's a full-time job. Defending one's self and one's nation is a very difficult task. Because I had that task called combat soldier, that's a story for another time and book. I am now honorably discharged out of the US Army, thank God, but now I am in God's army. I am a solider fighting on God's side and that's a very hard job, doing God's will every day, and I will do his will every second of my life every day that he gives me. And I am more than honored to do so. I felt so grateful to even be born. Many people were never even born. But yet, maybe in Heaven.

Genocide—the thought of murder for any reason. The thought of killing an entire race is hurtful to my heart, soul, and mind. Now I know why Jesus wept. He looked into man's future and wept. He saw years down the road. How the Jews were enslaved by the Egyptians, and how the Jews were put to death by the Germans. They used genocide procedures on them. How they took their valuables, from everything, from their homes, to the littlest babies, putting them in oven-like buildings and killing millions of them. To this day, much is written and spoke about these great hurtful and crying about sins. Man-on-man sins. The Jewish people have suffered much in the long life of mankind. The Jew has suffered in Germany so much as to be hunted down by name by the German government. Killed my Jews because of success in their lives. Our Father in heaven protects the Jewish nation and, thank God, always will the Jewish nation will be attacked and God's angels will attack back. The war will ensue. The war will be on. The last world war will be the last for mankind. The defense of the Jewish nation and people will be the last war on this earth. The battle of Armageddon will be fought with nuclear weapons by man, and God's angels will be using much more powerful weapons against mankind. And the sad part about all of this is that I'm reporting to all of mankind before this all takes place. I am warning you ahead of time. But yet and still, you, as a weak people, can't pray, won't pray, refuses to listen, refuses to turn from our wicked ways, so the earth will be destroyed by fire. We all will be judged and go our separate ways forever and ever. My name is Jimmy L. McLaurin, reporting my findings to you on this day of our Lord. I should have made this the last thing written, but no, I want to show this step by step until the final seconds of our Father's return.

It is reported that he will laugh at and mock man. He will make us feel so bad deep down inside for not heeding his orders, his word. We will see the world destroyed. We will see it literally go up in smoke. We will see much crying and dying everywhere. We will realize our greatest fears have arrived. We will see our time is truly up. The end of our unjust, unrighteous people. People in our family, hateful people on our streets, robbers, thieves, liars in our neighborhoods. Unjust lawyers, judges, congressmen, congresswomen, senator, doctors, CEO, hospital heads, owners of every lot. Vice presidents, presidents of every nation, people of all races known to man will watch. They all, we all will be helpless.

We will be under the mighty hand of our Father. Our time will be up. From that time on, man's time and control will be all over. The entire world will be under fire. The fire will be out of man's control. We all will be under our Father's command. We will have seen or saw the mighty Father at work. I feel it's much harder to build than it is to destroy, but it takes more time to create something. I feel you all should know the hard, cold truth, and I have given you some of it, but I have much, much more to say. I am a writer of today and tomorrow. So I have just begun my story of life. Please read on and help me get us through these times of building everlasting life. The planning of following in our Father's world, a life of goodness. Promise sharing, caring, giving, praying, having, asking, being heard, talked to, taught, cared about, addressed shown. And being greatly loved. All of these things and many, many more. I believe God has much more for mankind. He has things our eyes have not seen and our ears have not heard. I believe he has seas like no one we've ever seen. Lake and valleys, streets of gold cities not made by the hands of mankind, trees and plants that are grown in heaven, food that is made in heaven. Can you see the building that are made by the hands of an angel? Could you imagine how the food's taste made by an angel? Could you possibly imagine hearing a heavenly choir or even being in a heavenly choir? Can you even think about seeing your people that have been gone before you were born? The people that you just saw in pictures and photo albums? The people you've never saw? Can you imagine seeing Adam and Eve? Can you see Jesus Christ and hear all about his trials and tribulations on this earth? Would that be music to your ears? Would it not be great to hear the many stories of Jesus Christ, reliving his time here on earth? We all have hopes and people we all would love to hear from. From the smallest babes to the oldest person. People we deeply miss. People that we feel left us, or people we feel that were taken from us. People we feel we need. People we will never forget. I feel that these are treasures of our God's people, our Father's creations. God, the true Maker and Creator. He is the one that gave them to us. All the more reason for our thanks unto him. He is the master giver, and we are the receiver. It's kind of amazing to me how we, as human beings, cannot get the sin out of our lives down through time.

Family after family, we keep getting deeper and deeper into sinful ways and doing things. We have old people whom many call saints of God, people that I believe are living all that they know. And as the Bible says, go and sin no more, but beings are very weak. We are from the dust of the earth, and we shall return back to it. So I know as weak as we are, we have no excuses for our sins, a wrongdoing. We must study, write, read, listen, and learn. I would love to make a point here. The point about Adam and Eve, the people we all came from. If you look closely at the situation, Adam and Eve, I know, were not born. I know that Eve must have been a beautiful creature to look upon. She had to be stunning, and Adam had to be a superman. Now when you think about it, they, I believe, were built stronger than today's human beings. They lived much, much longer than we do today. And Adam, man of God, he gave every animal its own name, so he had to be very, very smart. He had years of knowledge. He lived on this earth for years now. This man and woman are very special unto this day. I would like to put this major league point out there. We must be more than aware that Satan is on earth doing his best to kill and destroy us as human beings. If he tricked our mother and dad who were aware of his wrongdoings and was told by our Father, who gave them warning from his own mouth, and they heard it, does that not put a chill down your spine to let you know how dangerous this Satan truly is? It literally puts a chill down my spine. I truly feel a great challenge getting this chilling news out to mankind by my writing and word of mouth, and to think about it, many people may have never heard the word *Satan*, the devil, the evil one, the sinful one. Many people don't even believe that evil exists. They don't believe in evil beings. They don't believe in spirits at all. So I know this is a huge challenge to be done. But it must be put out there for the good and victory of our people. We must win this war. We can't fail. We are all made by God. We are all his children. We are all loved by our Father in heaven. And as Jesus Christ said, I must be about my Father's business, and I hear his call, and now I am on my way. It's amazing to me how quiet the name *Satan* is. The people never ever mentioned his name much in public places. They are low-key. They are very quiet about the evil. It's not a secret.

Today or in the past, God made many people of every hue, color as the rainbow, every people of a world of differences. All made by him with his stamp of approval. And I love the fact that he gives us all a chance to go our own way in this life. God has never had a slave. God has never forced anyone to do his will. God has never made man pray to him. My God has never given us wrong teachings. God has always let us go our own way. But he let us know that his way is the only way. There are two ways: his way which is right and true, and the other way which is the wrong way. And as he says, the works, the job, the labor, the word wages is the money, the return for work. The rewards for what you have done. We call wages the wards for sin is truly death. People, I've got these hard-earned and hard-learned teachings. Please do listen. Check out my word, and you will agree with me. I am not the father of right and wrong, but my Father in heaven is. And like I said before, I got it hard-learned. He taught me through many tears, and my feelings being hurt but not destroyed. He let me know there is no other but him, that he is my Father, my Creator, my Maker, my bread, my water, my shelter, my heat on a cold winter day, my bathwater for bath, my bed, my breakfast, my lunch, my dinner, my snacks, my mother, my brother, my sister, my family, my friend, my lawyer, my judge. My house, my car, my doctor, my place of comfort, my pillow, my TV screen, my radio, my lover, my mouthpiece, my preacher, my peace of mind. I am a man that complains, and he lets me know when I do much complaining. I am telling him he is not doing a good job. He tells me to work harder to change the things you can change. And he never stops working. He will do his job as he has done from the beginning until the end. The same God that one day will even bring death to a death. He will stop and destroy even death. What a mighty God we must serve. His will be done. As Jesus Christ even said, not my will but your will be done, and at that, I must say I just can't stop praising his name. I just can't stop, won't stop. I feel I will be writing all about this the rest of the days of my life. It's like fire shut up in my bones. I must get this feeling inside of me out of me to the rest of all universes. It can't be stopped. How sweet it is. It raises my thought process. I raise my spirit. He's lifting me up to a higher level. My Father truly does a great work. He gives me ideas I know aren't from me. He walks with me. He talks with me, and he tells me I am his own. And that gives me a reason to keep on keeping on. I feel like living forever, and I say you are my Father in whom I am well pleased. People, long after I am dead and gone, these words will never die. These very words were here before I got here, but I just want you to know I believe every single word, and I am putting in the work through writing, and I have the faith. But I am putting in the work. Faith without work is dead. I have both faith and work, but I must push myself for much, much more of both. And in doing so, I must push you to get in our Father's loving army now! Please listen. As I was reading the newspaper today, as a matter of fact, *the Buffalo News* dated January 27, 2016, page A2. The title is "Doomsday Clock Inches Closer to Midnight."

On Thursday, a group of scientists who orchestrated the doomsday clock, a symbolic instrument informing the public when the earth is facing imminent disaster, moved its minute hand from 3 to 2.5 minutes before the final hour. It was the closest the clock had been to midnight since 1953, the year after the United States and the Soviet Union conducted competing tests of the hydrogen bomb. Though scientists decide on the clock's position, it is not a scientific instrument or even a physical one. The movement of its symbolic hands is decided upon by the science and security board of the bulletin of the atomic scientists.

The organization introduced the block on the cover of its June 1947 edition, placing at seven minutes to midnight. Since then, it has moved closer to midnight and further away depending on the board's conclusions. Skipping down in 1990 at the end of the Cold War, the clock was at ten minutes to midnight. The next year, it was a full 17 seventeen minutes away unchecked climate change, nuclear weapons. World leaders have failed to act with speed. These failures of political leaders endanger everyone on Earth is added.

After reading this article in the newspaper, I realize that many people know that our Father exists. And I know I must spread that knowledge for sure in the Holy Bible Acts 10:42–44, and the Bible says,

And he commanded us to preach unto the people and to testify that is he which was ordained of God to be the judge of the quick and the dead.

To him give all the prophets witness that through his name whosoever believeth in Him shall receive remission of sins. While Peter yet spoke these words, the Holy Ghost fell on all them which heard the word.

The Word sometimes refers to Jesus Christ. In the book of Philippians 1:2, it states, "Grace be to you and peace from God our father, and from the Lord Jesus Christ blessed be even the father of our Lord Jesus Christ." The father of mercies and the God of all comfort. Who comforted us in all our tribulations that we may be able to comfort them which are in trouble by the comfort wherewith we ourselves are comforted of God. For as the suffering of Christ abound in us, so our consolation also abounded in Christ. I say, as the Bible says, my conscience is to please our Father, and so far, I am far below even my own standards. So I beg of you. Please pray for me as I pray for you. Let's be about our Father's work. I must be about my Father's business, because in the end, it's the most important business of all. I've been told that the holy Bible is the basic instructions before leaving earth. And I feel I'm far behind my own schedule. The book of Revelations 2:18 states, "Unto the angel of the church in Thyatira write these things sayeth the son of God who hath his eyes like unto a flame of fire and his feet are like fine brass." That writing seems to be a man of color. Well, today is a new day to me. I just got up out of my bed, and I feel so free. It's took me years and decades for me to feel this way. I seldom felt safe in the good old US of A. But now that I look back on it. I usually was at work all day long, and at night, I had a second job. That I worked twice as strong. I was always a tired, young man because money in my life was greatly in demand. I never seemed to have enough. It always seemed like I needed more. The drive in me could never be filled because I had people all around me that was there will. I was told I could never be sick, and the people I worked with would say, unless you are dead, you can't be off the job, and they worked all the time and did their best to take every call. I know a lot of people that worked for at least fifty years, and I tried my best to seal that deal, but I got in a car crash. And that was that. It stopped me cold, cold in my tracks. I was in love with my career. I loved my job. It was a love that kept me going as if I was starving. I loved working sixteen hours every day, and for year and years, I would not have it any other way from the time I got up. I was on my way to work, and the time I left, I was on my way home. I was a slave to the job all my life. I worked from can't see in the morning until can't see at night, and never got tired of the heavy scheduled fight in fact. I got another job along the way.

Thank You God for Giving Us All a Chance at Eternal Life

The first job was a conductor on the railroad. Each and every day, I worked for all first-class railroad, all the day working my heart out. Long, hard, and strong. I loved the work and the people that worked with me. They were dedicated workers and believed we made a big difference in the world. I personally worked for Amtrak, Conrail, the Metro-North out of New York City. I worked for the CSX. I worked for many others. These people pushed me to high, high heights on the job. I qualified as a flagman from Canada to Boston, all over the East Coast of America. I usually got about two hours of sleep every night, and the people that worked with me felt it was more than a sin to miss out on work. And to be late was worse than bad. I remember working around the clock for days on end. We literally worked until we dropped. I recall working twenty-three-and-a-half hours at a time and have the company fined by the FFA for me working past the hours of service laws. I never got too much work or money. And I felt then as I do now. I thank my God for giving me the energy, the drive, the mind, and the will to keep on going. Even till this day, I am still going. Not strong, but thanks be to God I am still going forward, and now that I'm thinking about it, I would like to say thank you, fellow workers, for pushing me every day, keeping me working, getting paid, paying every day bills, keeping busy. At the start, I did not believe I could not make the first day, but day after day, week after week, year after year, I'm buried in their records. My name still lives somewhere in these records. And by the way, when I ever missed work, which was rare, the people would call my house to make sure I was still alive. By the way, the name is Jimmy L. McLaurin. I feel so good to tell this story because if I did not write it to you, this story could have never ever been told. And I thank our God for his inspiration and telling me to tell you I worked hard, and I mean very hard to let you know faith without works is truly dead, and that's the truth. You are hearing from me. I call myself Mr. Nobody for the first six years on the railroad. I was not known as the saying goes. I've been working on the railroad all the livelong day. And I am proud to say I loved every day.

My grandad worked on the railroad, he worked on the track gang back in the 1920s. He worked and lived in North Carolina. He seldom talked about work. But I know he worked very hard. He was a man of God, and he taught his daughter well, whom is my mother. My granddad was a superman, and his daughter was and still is a hero in my life. And my granddad is also a hero as well. I must tell you, many of my family members I view as heroes, they hung on in there until death did them part. I now know it's easy to die. But it takes a true champ to hang on in there regardless what comes and what goes. And I would like to say our Father in heaven filled my life with true champs. People that dealt with life every day. And it was tough. My people struggled. And had trouble come their way on a daily basis. They never let anything stop them, even the law was against them. They were treated bad and wrong for so, so long. That they knew that trouble don't last always. Any man born of a dark woman will have dark days, and I am a man born of a dark woman, and I must say I've had many dark days. But through all the fears, tears, jeers, lears, and hateful cheers, I still say my Father still sits on his throne.

He is still on his job. He is still yet alive. He is still King of kings and Lord of lords. He is still taking care of his businesses, and I am still and always will be his business, and I am so grateful and glad and proud to be his son, his servant, and one of his man worshipers. I know I don't deserve it, but I am one of his favored, one of his own. He hears my cry. He hears my voice. He sits more than high, but looks lower than low to hear my complaint. He is deeper than deep, more clear than clear. He is all over me. Every day of my life, I will give him praise. I was ordered by him in the book of Acts 10:42 to preach and testify about him and more and more I keep on doing his will, and I truly believe in his Word. In fact, the Bible tells me that the Word actually means Jesus Christ. It tells me that we must do God's will. Jesus actually says not my will, but your will be done. And I know Jesus being the Word. All he says is true. Jesus is responsible for all mankind yet living. He refused to let us be killed. They said to him, you can't save your own life yet, and still he died for all mankind. And many people are unaware of this fact, and it's not talked about publicly in most gatherings. Most people feel it's a private thing and not to be put on the spot. I've heard it said it's embarrassing and interfering with their private lives, and

I've even heard it said you are being nosey and to please keep your religious thoughts to yourself, and then you must know Satan's spirit is present, and I must let this fact be known. That every human being on earth will be attacked by the evil spirits of Satan. And the answer to that attack is to say the blood of Jesus. Say the blood of Jesus save me all through the attack. Keep saying save me by the blood of Jesus. In the name of Jehovah, please save me, and if you believe, he will rescue you. Works without faith is dead, and faith without works is dead. I've been attacked many times, but I used the tools called prayer and thank God they worked, and due to our God in heaven, I yet live. I count that a great thing. I have so much to tell you. I will be writing for the rest of my life, and I plan to write at least six or seven hundred more books. You see, I'm just getting started. My dad died about eleven years ago, and he told me, son, don't write a book until I am dead and gone. So I did as he requested. I've waited, and since he has passed, I plan to write hundreds of books and that's my job. And I feel the calling of my Father in heaven inspiring me on to put his truth out there. To let men and women know that in the beginning, he says seek him and to know right from wrong. It's a hard road, but truth shall set you free. I am not the author of right and wrong, but my Father in heaven is, and until my last breath, I will tell you. I have a point to be made in the book of Micah. Please don't wait until the end. Micah chapter 3:4 says,

> Then shall cry unto the Lord but he will not hear them: he will even hide his face from them at that time, as they have behaved themselves ill in their doings. Thus sayeth the Lord concerning the prophets that make my people err, that bite with their teeth, and cry, Peace.

I was guilty of much wrong. I got it hard enough and hard-learned. The Lord taught me through his love. For me, whom he loves, he will chastise, and he will press you. He will let you know he is the only way. He let me know. And I am more than grateful in the book of Corinthians. It makes it very clear. Second Corinthians 1:2–4 says,

> Grace be to you and peace from our father. And from the Lord Jesus Christ. Blessed be the God … [even]

the father of mercies and the God of all comfort, who comfort us in all our afflictions, that we may be able to comfort them which are in any trouble by the comfort wherewith we ourselves are comforted of God.

I write to you from the word of the Bible. I go to the. Verse 13 says, "For we write none other things unto you than what ye read or acknowledge and I trust ye shall acknowledge even to the end." I know that God is still on his throne working hard every day. He never takes a day off. He is always taking care of me when I look at all the miracles he has done in my life. He gave me a high school education. He gave me jobs to support me and my family. All through life, some jobs were hard, but they supplied the need at that time I've worked at least fifty different jobs. God gave me decent health, God gave me decent housing, God gave me money to buy good food. I've never been hungry a day in this lifetime. I've never lived outside except when I had a job in the US Army, and we did our job, which was at that time living outside, and even then, I felt living outside was a very hard way to live. And to think millions of people are homeless in this great county, the United States of America. I've witnessed men and women fighting over garbage cans. I've seen homeless people fighting over cardboard boxes, which they called their homes. They felt that the garbage cans were their refrigerator. They lived outside in alleys on the streets all over America. I've seen homeless people all over. I went to Las Vegas, Nevada, and they had an underground network even in Las Vegas, and I should not have been surprised, but I was. Many poor people of America live in Las Vegas, Nevada, and I saw it myself. The weather is good, very little snowfall, so that saves a lot of money. I live in the north east, better known as Western New York. In fact, where I live is called one of the poorest locations in America today. But I like the locality. It's very good for family and me. It's not too hot and not too cold. The people live good lives and are close to fair, not fair but close. They have good fences which makes for good neighbors. I'm usually busy, and I stay out of other people's business, so I am not nosy. So I do my best to stay out of trouble. Usually, trouble finds you. My dad had this interesting saying when he was yet alive. He used to say, a man can get into trouble two ways— starting and stopping. I find people have a multitude of ways of getting into trouble, and getting out of trouble is a total new book. I've heard so many stories about troubles. It amazes even me. I love this life, and I still complain, but I know when I complain, I'm telling my God he's not doing a great job. But the fact of the matter is, he's doing a great job. It's me that's doing the bad job. I'm the one that's got to get on my job and do much better. I feel I can do much better. I used to say I'm wasting time, but the truth is, you are wasting yourselves because you never can get that time back. And that's a sad fact. I wanted to tell you so much more, but my pages are getting few. I've got a lot more to tell you. I studied the Jewish religion, and the old Jewish thought was that Jesus Christ was a spokesman.

And the common thought was that he was not the son of God. They felt that he was born of Mary, whom later married Joseph, whom had children. The leaders of the Jewish religion did not believe in his divine birth. They knew the story but did not believe the man. He had hair like sheep's wool. The man had eyes like flames of fire. The man had feet like brass. The man was humble, kind, and spoke beyond his years. The man had brothers and sisters that did not follow him, and in his own hometown, his own village, his own people did not believe in him, did not trust him, and were not with him. Isn't that how you are viewed by many of your family members, many of your so-called friends, many of your townsfolk, many of your coworkers, many of your city folks? Isn't that funny? You think about it, and you can relate much more closely than you would care to take a close look. This happened over two thousand years ago. And if you take a look at yourself and you can take it personally or not but the end result will be the same on a mental scale, I'm pretty sure the people would not hurt no more than your feelings. Because they don't feel like wasting all that time to make you famous by making you a martyr. We are not important to many people. Most people in your neighborhood have no idea who you are, and the fact of the matter is, most don't know you, and even fewer want to know you or your family and that's an American fact. We've grown so far from family and those few friends we have. Lack of trust and lack of faith has put us in a state of belief. We lost trust in people, family, friends, all governments on every scale, and in a lot of cases for good reasons. We, the people, are being taken advantage of. You answer the phone, some scam artist, some robber, some crook could be calling. It's amazing how easy they get your phone number. They may be correct.

The computer age has arrived. The age of know-how, the age of knowledge is here. But along all the information, so is the better thief, the better robber, all in one and the same. Along with the better rapist, the better liar, the better killers. Man with all his knowhow is getting weaker and wiser, and his march to the end is getting closer as time goes on. We live in great times. We, as human beings, have made great gains. We, as a people, have overcome much. We are steady moving forward unchecked. We need to start checking ourselves, our children, our schools, our family, our home. Our neighborhoods, our streets. We need to check our local officials. Me included. I do a poor job of checking all these politicians. I lead the way in neglect as far as checking on politicians' records and what they are doing in my neighborhood. What they say, what they do, who they represent in the background. I don't know, but I certainly need to because there are many secrets right in our faces, and we need to correct much of this wrongdoing because wrong is wrong. Let's get these people doing wrong gone. Out of office, out of power, and out of our pockets. They have been getting our money for far too long. Our job is to make this a better world, and we can help by getting rid of every crook out of office and across America. We have more than we will ever need. It is up to me to at least make you aware. I am not doing a good job, but I am trying to get on it. I fell a time or two, but I got up. I've been tricked a time or two, but I catch on quickly.

These people are smart, full of guile, wicked, worldly, and more than evil. And believe me, many, and I mean many evil, wicked, smart people are very, very rich. That's a good thing to remember. Question oneself if this person is rich and how so. How and by what means did they get rich, and believe me, a lot of the time it will take you down a long road that you won't like, but we are all looking to be safe and comfortable. Not all people want to be rich but satisfied. And for many people, that is more than good. I've been working hard most of my life. I'm not rich, but being close to comfortable. I got a new job working for you as a writer. I was told by my dad to don't write anything until after he is dead. Well, he's been dead for over a decade, and I want to be a writer, and I count it a blessing because I would have only wrote one book, and now I feel I'll now write hundreds of books. I retired off one job, so now I'm starting a new career, and I see I love it already. And I always say I got to ninety, at least sixty more years. I've got one hundred more years of work from this 2017, but I'll get one hundred years, but I know I put in more than one hundred years of work already. But life and death is in the tongue, and I speak life all day, every day, and I won't give up the ghost happily until I'll do my Father's will. My dad on earth is dead and gone, but I hope to write about him and his life to carry on his legacy before I'm gone. But first, I must write about my Father in heaven, the King of kings and Lord of lords, before I leave this earth. I must speak his Word and truth. Before I go anywhere, I must be about my Father's business, so I got sixty more years to handle it. But I must carry on as if today is my last day here.

I find it very interesting to note that the Bible mentions genealogy and birthrights. It was explained to me years ago that Moses had a staff, and the staff had his people's name written on it, and that I noticed that the staff was put on the ground and turned into a snake. The fact that the Bible mentions that is very important to me. I see that the Bible is up-to-date even in this day and time. It says that there is nothing new under the sun, and I wonder, did man have any outside help from the elite beings because I know we would be more than ignorant to believe we are in this universe alone. There is so much going on in our world. Can you imagine what is going on in other worlds? It's truly something to discuss and something to think about. Most people fear other beings, but the question should be asked, are we feared or pitied? It may be both. Is man that evil? Are we that wicked that other being run from us, hide from us, avoid us literally, and duck us? I feel the place is far too large, much too big for us to be here all alone, and I truly know the people working for NASA space stations keep much from the average citizen. They know if we knew what was really going on, we would have much fear in our hearts and minds. We are kept in the dark. People know things and see things and don't say a word to anyone. My people see things and know things, but no one wants the troubles that you can get just by telling what you saw. People are scared all over the world. They live and die in fear. They go out scared, come in scared. They go to work fearful, go to the banks scared. They go shopping terrified, and the people with guns are at an all-time high. People are looking for protection, safety, security, and comfort. People are insecure. They see TV, the news, and they want police protection, and I'm not so sure about police anymore. The police in some case or on the take and that's in question every day. I see racial tensions a lot on the TV. The news media is a great influence in today's world. The news is a great thing in people's lives. We all want to know what is happening in our world. And the news media is doing their jobs pretty well. The new things out there are just fantastic like the computers. The information travels around the globe in minutes, and I personally think that's a great thing, but the question is, are all the reports true? The news media makes a lot of reports, a lot of money, and I question, do they make a lot of mistakes? That's a big question. I know a lot of people like President Trump question the news often, and the man may be correct. Nahum chapter 1 verse 2: "God is jealous and the Lord revengeth." The next verse, verse 3 says, "The Lord is slow to anger and great in power and will not at all acquit the wicked. The Lord hath his way in the whirlwind and in the storm and the clouds are the dust of his feet. He rebunketh the sea and maketh it dry."

I understand that the Lord actually corrects the sea. He speaks to the water and makes it behave. And I know that the sea can be twelve miles deep, at least as high as any mountain. I find it amazing that when God destroyed the earth with the flood, you seldom read anything about the water life. Not much spoken about the fish of the water. The mention of the large whales. At that time, the animals of the sea must have been truly thriving. No man to destroy the fish population. In fact, I've heard it said some scientists believe that whales can communicate from the Atlantic Ocean to the Pacific Ocean, and it's a disagreement at how old a whale can live. And I read but I wonder if a whale ever stops growing. I read where some scientists believe they keep on growing until death. So more than likely, man has never seen the biggest whales, and with the seas being so vast and much of it under ice, it leaves much to the imagination. There's truly a lot to this, but we keep on learning new things. Our tech is getting better, and to keep up with the old as well as the new, it needs to get much better. I've been thinking about many things. Especially about the things as far as the sea like space travel and the space stations. The Bible says there is nothing new under the sun that brings to mind. For me, anyway. The space travel of mankind today and all the news about UFOs and how these people are working for NASA that try their best to get in touch with other worlds and the world's space teams. I see things in the Bible about other mansions. In my Father's house are many mansions, and if it were not so, I would have told you. The fact that it's in the Bible, it piques my never-dying interest. I study. I want to know what is going on in that great beyond, that great unknown. And I just keep on digging until I uncover the truth or at least as I can come to the truth. Because I believe that as far as UFOs go, I'm more than sure a lot is being hidden from me, and I want to know the facts, the truth. However, I know the truth and the facts by man's standards can be totally different. I found that out, but that's a driving force in my life. My mind wants to know not everything, but a lot more than I now know. The Bible says I destroy my own people for lack of knowledge and don't want to be destroyed for lack of knowledge. I want to know, and not only do I want to know, but I also want to write down what I know and have others read what I write to them so they can tell the world. There is an old song, it goes like this: "Tell me the stories of Jesus I love to hear … Scenes by the wayside, tales of the sea. Stories of Jesus, tell them to me." I reported it's legendary over two thousand years ago. Jesus Christ and his disciples would be seen a far off by the children. They would see him and run to him in huge groups, and they would plead with him to tell them all of the wonderful stories of his more-than-awesome life. He would sit around campfires and tell these little ones all about heaven. Remember, he saw all of heaven, and who was and is still there. He saw the streets of gold. He saw and heard the heavenly choir. He is a witness to all that went on in heaven. And he came back to earth to report to the children all that he had seen and heard, and I would like to report to this day that song is still sung. And that's been over two thousand years ago. And I would love to say our Savior and his and our Father is still sitting on that throne. And he is my Father in whom I am well pleased. These are facts of life our Father who is in heaven sent his beloved Son Jesus Christ, whom yet lives, who will do all the Bible says. It is amazing to me how the Bible is written five hundred years. It took more than five hundred years to complete the Holy Bible. The Word could not be stopped. God made sure that we would get the chance and the opportunity to receive his Word, and time and place would arrive for us. People, one by one, would get our chance to get a look at his book, his Word. His will be done on earth as it is in heaven. A small fact to remember: there is no darkness in heaven, so there is no evil spirits in heaven. So there is darkness on earth, and there are evil spirits on earth. We are challenged a lot on earth. We are in a fight much of the time with these demons, and one thing for sure, please don't play with the board of evil—Ouija boards. They are of the devil. They are wicked. Please remember that.

I am not famous. I not well–known. I have no following. I don't pastor or preach at no one's church. I've never held any public or private office. Never been in any political arena of any kind. Never been on any debate team. Never even ran for dog catcher. Never been on anyone's political team. Never been a thief or a liar convicted in any court for any crime. Never been convicted of any crime, but thanks be to Jesus Christ, an innocent man, a honest man, a God-fearing man, the son of God straight out of heaven. A man that wept for us. A man clean. A loving man. More than a good man. A man that raised the dead. A man that calmed the raging sea. A man that turned water into wine. A man that healed the very sick. A man that fed the hungry. A man that helped the brokenhearted. A great teacher. A man that wept over all mankind. A man that made it possible for me to go and be in heaven with him and his family. A man that had a job. A man that worked with his own hands. A man that spoke to men, women, as well as children. A man of incredible understanding. A fearless man. A man that had mother, brothers, sisters. A man that was and still is more than humble, more than true, more than honest. More than faithful, more than loyal, more than kind, more than forgiving. A man more than giving. A man more than charitable. A man closer than a friend, closer than a brother. A man that gave of himself. I feel, and you should know, a man that never sinned yet and still this man was convicted to being called a liar. Being convicted as king of the Jew. Yet and still, the leaders of the Jewish faith were the ones calling for his death. A man convicted in their courts of law. They didn't believe he was the Son of the most high God. They talked badly to him. They spat on him. They hit him with stones in the streets. They laughed at him. They hurt his feelings. They hurt his body. They hurt his mind. They put him in prison, and they held him there. They were breaking their own laws. They brought him before trials late at night, which was said to be against the Jewish law. They beat him all about his body while not yet found guilty. They gambled for his clothes. They came to the wrong chooses, but it was meant to be. He paid the price for you and me to go totally free. Our debt was paid free in clear. He was crucified on the tree. You see, he paid the highest of high prices for you and me. He is said to have not spoken a mumbling word, knowing all the time the angels were in heaven, watching and listening for the "come save me" word, but he took all of it like the champ he is and gave a wonderful chance to keep on living. He did not fight back or seek revenge. He just let mankind keep on living. If he would have yelled for help, we would never been born, not one of us. But being the one that my Father said, "This is my beloved Son in whom I am well pleased," he has given us another chance to go our many ways. I beg of you to make sure it's the right way for our lives are short. We are cut down like a blade of grass, and in one hundred years, how many of us will last? Death is for sure a thing that will come, but that's the short of it. That's where it will only begin. Because after you die, you must go somewhere, and that place is up to you. So I pray to God above that you know what to do. I pray for your soul. More and more because I'm getting much smarter as I go. I'm getting older and more read. I feel I must learn much more before I am dead. I do not have much time in my life because I was a poor man. Most of the time I was always busy working a job or two, and I always had a lot of things to do. I prayed when I had the time, and that was never enough. My life was never really that tough. I kept on moving as I still do today, and my Father in heaven always makes a way.

I tell you now and never forget. Everyone gets their chance, so don't forget. I've come a long hard way, and every day, if you are around me, you will hear me say thank you, God. I yet live another day. I am more than grateful, and I know I don't deserve your mercy or your love, so please give me more time before you take me home high above. I'm in no hurry to get there. Please let me stay here some more time so I can help the people in my life. They need help. And I'm doing my best to help them get ready before you call me to rest. They don't realize who you are, and I want to let them all know before they go too far off course, as many people do. Because I know they can't survive without you. From Israel to Rome to Egypt to France and beyond, man can't make a step without your guidance. We are lost without you, and that's the fact. Without you, we can never get back. We are made from the dust of the earth, and dust is very weak. I know firsthand. We go our way every day, but it seems like we are lost most of the way. We usually get it wrong no matter how hard we try. We are mankind, a weak creature no matter how hard we try, but thank you, Father, for never leaving us alone. Thank you so much for being so strong. In all our lives, you show up. We are not smart enough to know that you are there. We think we are doing it all ourselves. We are people, and we don't know how weak we are in your world. It's so vast, so big. We live our lives and only get a small glance of what's really going on. Before we know, we are long dead and gone. I'm looking and studying about the past and all the lost arts of the long-ago past. We lost a lot along the way, but I'm studying each and every day. I've had a lot of smart people in my life, and I get a lot of information all along the way, but I always feel I can learn much more along this life's highway.

My favorite book that I love to read is the Holy Bible. It's the most important for me. My loving mother, she used to read her Bible, the Word, every single day. She was a saint in my day and age. She would be praying for her family both night and day, and she went to church every Sunday. She would go to church five to six times a week and said to me, "Son, I don't want to see you weak, so pray and read God's Word and do his work." Well, I was favored. I now know that's a fact. My people prayed for me, and I feel the Lord's calling on me now. I'm writing the things he gives to me. I have to put his Word and his will out there. I can't die and leave this world without at least sharing with you the words of God. I know in my soul, my heart, my spirit. I know it to be true. I had someone pray for me. And I know I must pray for you in order for you to make it through, so it goes far beyond family and some would say friend. I must say, please remember your family and most of all our Father in heaven, who has his arms outstretched day and night, begging for us all to do what he says is true and right, and the grace of Jesus Christ be with you all. Amen.

About the Author

J. L. McLaurin, a man of God. Educated as a conductor on all class I Railroad, Amtrak, Metro-North, CSX, Southern Railway, and a few others.

CPSIA information can be obtained
at www.ICGtesting.com
Printed in the USA
BVHW08s0133180918
527751BV00001B/17/P

9 781642 582437